BRITISH RAIL
TRACTION
MAINTENANCE DEPOTS
1974–1993

Part 2: Central & Southern England

MICHAEL RHODES

Published by Platform 5 Publishing Ltd,
52 Broadfield Road, Sheffield, S8 0XJ. England.

Printed in England by The Amadeus Press, Cleckheaton, West Yorkshire.

ISBN: 978 1 915984 02 9

Above: 20190 and 20037 are stabled at the front of a packed line-up at the northern end of Toton depot on 13 March 1980. What appears to be a father, along with his two prospective rail enthusiast children, can be seen making their way from the colourful car park to the adjacent shed building. This view was taken from the artificial bank created to the east of the Toton complex in 1948, when the new 12-track reception yard for the Up Hump Yard was created, carving into what had been a gentle sloping hillock.

Front cover: These were just some of the locos that could be seen at Toton depot on 5 July 1987, when the red stripe variant of British Rail's Railfreight livery was the dominant branding. Members of Classes 08, 20, 31, 47, 56 and 58 are all visible and there are a few more locos out of sight on the left.

Back cover: On Friday 29 July 1983, 37270, 46028 and 45038 bask in the Cornish sun after having been parked up at St Blazey depot.

Previous page: Tibshelf Sidings were adjacent to the main line between Chesterfield and Alfreton, the edge of which is just visible on the extreme left of this view. On 10 July 1984, a variety of diesels could be found in the sidings and from left to right these are 56066 at the front of a rake of loaded MGR wagons, 20047 & 20150 and 58008 which was only a few months old at the time. 58014 was also present that day.

CONTENTS

INTRODUCTION

Many of us remember the halcyon days of trainspotting in the 1970s and 1980s. Steam may have gone, but there was still the excitement that the large variety of motive power brought and the "Locoshed Directory" published by Ian Allan to encourage us to seek out the locomotives that could be found on shed. We called it "shed bashing" back in 1972. We never had a permit and we always sought the best advice as how to "bunk" the shed and collect all the numbers. It seems madness in today's health & safety, woke and politically correct world but it was a wonderful time.

As a school boy living in South Wales, for me Saturdays were all about trainspotting. Would we go to Cardiff for the morning, or if we had saved enough money from our paper round to have a day out, we would get up early and head somewhere more exotic. By exotic, I mean anywhere outside South Wales! Favourite trips were a day to London to visit the sheds at Stratford and Finsbury Park, and then maybe Old Oak Common or Hither Green before a late train home. The commonest trip we made was north to Derby for Toton depot and this was sometimes combined with a trip to Tinsley in Sheffield, or to Bescot and Saltley in the Midlands. On three occasions, these trips coincided with Derby Works open day and another long but enjoyable day out was to Crewe Works open day, which was a high point in the calendar.

In addition to depots where both repairs and refuelling took place, there were many stabling points dotted about the country. Some of these had more locomotives on site than the major depots did. Stabling points were also the key to tracking down elusive shunting locomotives and the 1973 publication "Shunter Duties" by the Inter City Railway Society was an invaluable aid for doing this. The aim of every trainspotter in the 1970s was to "clear" British Rail (BR), meaning to see every locomotive, or indeed every locomotive, diesel multiple unit (DMU) and electric multiple unit (EMU). I managed to clear BR in 1978 when I finally saw 25321 on Carlisle's Kingmoor depot! Of course clearing BR was a moving target, as new stock was introduced and older locomotives were withdrawn. By the summer of 1978 however, my interest was increasingly focussed on photography and much less

on number collection, so much so that from 1980 I recorded what I photographed in my notebooks but no longer recorded every locomotive I saw.

The reader might well ask why the period from 1974 to 1993 has been chosen. Its start was dictated by the time I began photographing depots and its end was determined by several factors. Concerns about trespassing were becoming greater as we entered the 1990s. At the same time I was no longer a student or junior doctor, but was working as a lecturer in Surgery in Cardiff from 1992 and I was concerned that getting arrested for visiting an engine shed would be irresponsible. Palisade fencing was also appearing around depots and I can remember finding entry into Canton and Immingham suddenly being impossible due to the new fencing. The tradition of "shed bashing" was accepted as normal in the 1960s, tolerated in the 1970s and had turned into trespass with consequences by the early 1990s.

In the first book of this three-part collection, which covered the many depots and stabling points of Northern England that always seemed to be packed with locomotives, I dipped into my photograph collection to share a variety of images. This is the second volume in the series. It covers Southern & Central England and the final volume will examine the sheds of Wales and Scotland. The series is not a text book or historical summary of all the depots, but rather a recollection of hundreds of hours of a misspent youth. Some major depots hardly feature because I made few visits to them or didn't take any photographs there. Two such major sites are Finsbury Park and Stewarts Lane. On the other hand, my "home" depots, such as March Whitemoor and Gateshead (in the previous book) are perhaps over represented because I lived near these at different times. Hopefully this selection of images will bring back many happy memories for those of us who enjoyed the freedoms of trainspotting in the 1970s and '80s.

Michael Rhodes
Thurston, 2023

CENTRAL ENGLAND

BARROW HILL

We begin with Barrow Hill, which lies at the northern end of the Central England region. The depot and roundhouse were built in 1870 and serviced freight locomotives continuously until 1991. After closure, the buildings came perilously close to demolition, until they were granted Grade II listed status in 1991. The site was eventually purchased by Chesterfield Borough Council in 1996 and reopened as a museum in 1998. The Locoshed Directory reminded me that Barrow Hill was one of two depots which were quite a challenge to visit, the other being Shirebrook. After boarding a bus at the Chesterfield station approach, it was a 25-minute journey to Barrow Hill. This was the way I reached the depot for my early visits, but once at University, visits were made by bicycle and as I recall, the ride from Chesterfield or Worksop was quite hilly. Finally in the late 1980s and early 1990s, visits to the shed were made by car.

Class	Locos on 26 July 1974	Locos on 8 January 1977
03	03389	03189
08	08141, 08311, 08870 & 08871	08141, 08267, 08331, 08509, 08861, 08868, 08870 & 08871
20	20058, 20091, 20061, 20143 & 20169	20007, 20010, 20023, 20033, 20059, 20060, 20091, 20098, 20119, 20131, 20204 & 20209
25	25002, 25213 & 25254	None
31	31140, 31206 & 31284	None
37	37088	37120
47	None	47174, 47281, 47295, 47307 & 47316
56	None	56014 & 56015

Table 1: Locos present at Barrow Hill on two dates in the mid-1970s.

Above: On 8 January 1977 amongst the 29 locomotives present were 56014 and 56015. They had only arrived from Romania a couple of days earlier on the Harwich train ferry and still had the plywood packaging in place that had been used to protect them during transit. They were subsequently taken to Tinsley for testing and added to the freight fleet there. 08141 is parked alongside them at the turntable. Table 1 includes the full list of locomotives that were present that day, which was much more than the average weekend haul of between 10 and 15 engines.

Above: On 11 July 1984, 56015 and 56099 stand alongside 20129 and 20107. This view was taken looking away from the roundhouse, towards the spur which linked the depot to the main line at Barrow Hill Junction.

Above: In the late 1980s, locomotives would increasingly be stabled outside the roundhouse, as can be seen here on 11 July 1988. On the left are 20117, 20065, 20157 and 20128, whilst to the right are 56005, 56079, 58014 and 58013.

Above: By the summer of 1990 the depot at Barrow Hill was virtually deserted and closure was just months away. On 4 July 1990 a solitary 58044 was the only locomotive on shed. The collapse of the local coal industry rendered the depot surplus to requirements.

SHIREBROOK

The depot at Shirebrook was not one I often visited because it involved a 45-minute bus journey from Chesterfield, making it virtually a day out on its own! The diesel depot was effectively a replacement for Langwith Junction steam shed and was responsible for the many coal diagrams in north Nottinghamshire. The two-road maintenance shed opened in 1965 and survived until 1996 when the depot closed, largely as a result of the collapse of the local coal industry. The building still stands today, although it has been disconnected from the rail network and is now in commercial use. A major stabling point linked to Shirebrook was Worksop, which was also affected by the ravages of the decline in the coal industry. Worksop remained active after the closure of Shirebrook in 1996, but its demise was inevitable, as one by one the last of the area's collieries closed. The depot closed as a Network Rail facility in 2015 but has since been revived by Harry Needle Railroad Company. Table 2 shows a typical line up that could be found at Shirebrook depot on a weekend during the mid-1970s.

Class	Locos
08	08022, 08128, 08197, 08287, 08429, 08537 & 08778
20	20020, 20021, 20056, 20060, 20200 & 20202
25	25013, 25019, 25035 & 25064
37	37127, 37134, 37140 & 37170
47	47166, 47167, 47174, 47276, 47279, 47282, 47294 & 47316

Table 2: Locos present at Shirebrook on 26 July 1974.

Above: In the midst of the miners' strike, on 11 July 1984, 56030, 56115, 56008, 56113 and 56098 are stabled on the branch to Warsop Main Colliery, behind the depot at Shirebrook. The branch line was often used for storing locomotives during weekends but during the miners' strike they often remained there through the week.

Above & below: On 3 May 1990, Shirebrook shed was host to (from left to right) 58026, 58041, an unidentified Class 58, 56020, 20210 and 20214 which are partially obscured, an unidentified Class 56 on the Warsop branch and finally 58029. The upper image is a close-up of 58034 and 20210 & 20214 in the refuelling and minor repairs shed at Shirebrook.

Above: On 13 November 1990, the yard pilot at Worksop, 08813, stands outside the former diesel servicing shed. By 1990 the building had been completely given over to wagon maintenance as can be seen in this view, with quite a number of Merry-go-round (MGR) coal hoppers on site.

TOTON

Throughout the diesel era, Toton has held the crown for the depot where most locomotives could be found during weekends. Back in 1972, we heard stories about this depot, indicating it had double the number of locomotives that were present on my local depot, Cardiff Canton. In 1973, I made my first visit there, catching the No. 45 bus from Derby and alighting in Sandiacre. Over the two decades that this book covers, I found the staff at Toton to almost always be welcoming. On the dates that the nearby Derby Works held an open day Toton made a couple of staff available to act as unofficial guides, to keep an eye on the many enthusiasts who would inevitably turn up to look round because of the attraction of the nearby works open day.

Completed in 1965, the depot had a single 15-track building. Roads 1 to 4 were for refuelling and inspections whilst the roads numbered 5 to 15 were for heavy maintenance. During most of the last five decades the depot has been responsible for maintaining over 200 locomotives. Initially in the 1970s, this was mainly Class 20s and Class 45s (some of which were passenger locomotives for the services from Sheffield, Derby and Nottingham to St Pancras). In the 1980s, Class 56s and 58s arrived in large numbers and in the 1990s the depot looked after a fleet of Class 60s. With the arrival of English Welsh & Scottish Railway (EWS) and its fleet of Class 66s, the depot was initially responsible for all of this large new class. During the 1970s and '80s there were major stabling points linked to Toton at Nottingham, Westhouses and Burton-on-Trent. Two sample observations from visits during the 1970s can be seen in Table 3.

Class	Locos on 7 January 1974	Locos on 5 August 1978
08	3029, 3044, 3362, 3996, 08627 & 08929	08045, 08181, 08292, 08354, 08399, 08829, 08858, 08892 & 08894
20	8014, 8016, 8032, 8037, 8044, 8045, 8066, 8068, 8070, 8071, 8072, 8073, 8076, 8082, 8083, 8092, 8137, 8143, 8147, 8154, 8160, 8162, 8163, 8165, 8167, 8174, 8175, 8176, 8183, 8187, 8192, 8193, 8197 & 20080	20004, 20016, 20068, 20090, 20106, 20135, 20151, 20153, 20160, 20171, 20172, 20180, 20185, 20187, 20193, 20195 & 20198
25	5245, 5249, 5272, 5287 & 7664	25106, 25127, 25130, 25137 & 25268
31	5662 & 5800	31214 & 31269
37	6753	None
40	None	40014
44	1, 2, 3, 7, 8, 9 & 10	44002, 44004, 44007, 44008 & 44009
45–46	21, 24, 62, 74, 95, 97, 98, 100, 104, 115, 121, 126, 131, 134, 137 & 45113	45062, 45069, 45071, 45073, 45075, 45120, 45124, 45125, 45145 & 45147
47	1768, 1813, 1816 & 1854	47281, 47317, 47321, 47324, 47327, 47365 & 47366
56	None	56031, 56032, 56035, 56037 & 56041

Table 3: Locos present at Toton on two dates during the 1970s.

Above & below: These two views were taken from the same spot on the embankment of the A52 overbridge at Toton. They were captured using a 135mm lens which just allowed the full width of the depot complex to fit in the frame. Firstly, on 5 August 1978, when the weather was conducive to photography, the breadth of the depot and variety of traction is evident. Table 3 gives a list of what was present at the depot that day. The lower image is from 5 July 1987 and the change in motive power is very evident, with the more powerful Class 56s and 58s making up the majority of the locomotives on shed.

Above: Class 44s 44004 and 44005 stand alongside 45008 on 18 January 1977 while another "spotter" assiduously notes down the numbers to the right of the Class 45. The ten Class 44s spent most of their lives hauling coal trains, initially to Wellingborough and Brent Sidings in London and towards the end of their lives in the late 1970s more locally to power stations that were not equipped for MGR traffic such as Willington. They also handled mixed goods traffic to Whitemoor, Tinsley and Bescot, but rarely ventured further away from Toton than these three major marshalling yards.

Below: 20048 stands at the head of a row of Class 20s on the afternoon of Saturday 8 January 1977. Behind it are 20081, 20045, 20073, 20030, 20037, 20163, 20077, 20175 and 20169. This was a day when Derby Works held an open day and dozens of spotters were roaming around Toton that afternoon.

Above: The front ends of all the major classes allocated to Toton are seen here, looking across the northern end of the main shed at Toton on 8 January 1977. 47186 and 31138 are unfortunately the only locomotives I am able to confidently identify, as my notes from this visit are a bit vague and I recorded a total of 96 locomotives on shed.

Above: On 5 August 1978, which was another Derby Works open day, 44007 stands outside Toton. To its left are 44004 and 44002. There were 77 locomotives on shed that day.

Above: On 13 March 1980, I had arranged an official visit to Toton depot and yard on behalf of the Cambridge University Railway Club (CURC). Several members of the club can be seen walking past 45116, which is clearly in need of a wash! Behind it are 47325 and 45072, whilst to the right is the nose of 45130.

Right: The western end of the massive shed at Toton has 11 dead end roads for heavy maintenance. Here, on 13 March 1980, eight of these are seen from inside the depot with 56051 nearest the camera.

Above: These four images were taken on 2 July 1985 when I was working in Worcester. My notes suggest I took a day's holiday and left Worcester very early to get to Toton for 07.30. This first image shows the sun almost on the front of the depot in the morning, meaning it was indeed early! 25205 heads north from the down yard with the 6T64 trip working to Metal Box at Sutton-in-Ashfield. Behind, the depot is busy with Classes 20, 25, 45, 47, 56 and 58 all being present.

Above: 25151 has had a bad accident – ouch! On 3 September 1982 it was hauling the 8E08 Oakleigh to Barnby Dun (a train which only the year before had run via the Woodhead route and was hauled by Class 76s). The driver reported that he lost control on the descent to Huddersfield and he was diverted into Hillhouses Yard in Huddersfield, where the train crashed. The driver and guard were able to jump free before the impact damage was caused. Eventually the locomotive ended up at Toton where it was used for re-railing exercises until 1987.

Left & below: These two images of the northern end of the maintenance depot show 20029 and 45127 jacked up off their bogies, alongside 45150. In both images the engineers can be seen wearing makeshift headgear consisting of tied handkerchiefs and it is assumed that this is to protect their heads from dripping oil when they work on locomotives.

Left: This view of the heavy maintenance area at Toton was taken on 30 June 1987 and shows 20151, 20210 and 20161 standing in a row with 20001 to their left.

Below: By 27 December 1989, the new order was very much in evidence at Toton. This portrait of the south end of the depot shows the five through roads. The four sidings on the left were the refuelling and inspection tracks. From left to right are 20102 with at least two classmates, 60001, 58050 and 60006.

Below left: On 13 March 1980, 44004 looks to have had a minor prang as it sits next to newcomer 56058.

Above: On 10 July 1984, Nottingham depot was still busy in spite of the miners' strike and there were various members of Classes 20, 25, 47 and 56 on the shed. 08894 heads west past the depot, where many of the sidings are clearly designated for diesel multiple units (DMUs). It is engaged upon a trip freight from the goods depot to Nottingham Yard, which is to the west of Nottingham Midland station. Table 4 gives an idea of the variety of locomotives that could be found on the depot almost a decade earlier.

Class	Locos
08	08045, 08181 & 08856
20	20009, 20038, 20040, 20062, 20074, 20081, 20173 & 20185
25	25023, 25081, 25121, 25134 & 25218
40	40128
45	45101 & 45107
47	47076, 47285 & 47301

Table 4: Locos present at Nottingham on 27 August 1975.

Above right: On 12 March 1982, 20163, 20166, 20159 & 20193 are stabled at Westhouses depot. The shed, complete with many visible remnants of the steam era, would close within a year, when stabling would be transferred to the neighbouring Tibshelf Sidings.

Right: Between 1984 and 1987 Tibshelf became the northerly stabling point for Toton's locomotives. This general view of the yard was taken on 10 July 1984, which was during the miners' strike when levels of traffic were lower.

DERBY WORKS

Just a ten-minute walk from Derby station, the works at Derby held open days once or twice a year and as this selection of images shows, these were very well attended. The works had a close association with the Class 44, 45 and 46 "Peaks" from when the first of these was built there in 1959 to the last major repair in 1987. By the time of the last Class 45 repair, the Works was on its last legs and closed completely in 1990. The land which it occupied is now covered by the Pride Park Industrial Estate and Derby County's football stadium. Table 5 summarises a typical array of the motive power found at an open day during the mid-1970s.

Class	Locos
08	08043, 08068, 08074, 08176, 08182, 08225, 08328, 08349, 08397, 08399, 08454, 08455, 08493, 08507, 08666, 08739, 08885, 08905, 08909, 08927 & 08936
20	20021, 20031, 20062, 20063, 20129, 20212 & 20228
24	24034
25	D7524, 25030, 25045, 25058, 25061, 25065, 25069, 25073, 25097, 25106, 25113, 25123, 25125, 25154, 25173, 25236, 25243, 25287, 25296 & 25315
44	44001 & 44003
45	45009, 45013, 45023, 45034, 45039, 45047, 45048, 45051, 45053, 45055, 45102, 45115, 45130, 45139, 45142 & 45150
46	46004, 46008, 46038, 46051, 46053 & 46055
56	56017

Table 5: Locos present at Derby Works on 8 January 1977.

Below, above right and right: These three images were taken at the open day on 8 January 1977. 45150 stands under the engine testing building, 20063 is receiving attention in the main erecting shop after a variety of its components have been removed and 45015 rests beside seven classmates in the main works building. Unlike during the 1978 open day, I tried not to include the crowds in these images.

A second visit to Derby Works Open Day on 5 August 1978 yielded quite a number of photographs. It is wonderful to see the range of humanity at the day out, from wives in their finest to earnest trainspotters, all roaming unfettered round the works; oh and nobody got injured!

Left: 56045, which had only recently entered traffic, stands alongside a new High Speed Train (HST) power car at the works entrance, as two ladies watch on.

Below: 46007 is in pristine "ex-works" condition and is ready to leave the Works after a major overhaul.

Above: 44005 is under overhaul and has not yet regained its nose. The panoply of rail enthusiasts wandering around the works is a joy to behold in the days when there was a much more pragmatic approach to visitors and health & safety.

Above: RDB 968007, which was the departmental number given to the former 24061, is surrounded by crowds at the open day.

DERBY ETCHES PARK

A small diesel servicing depot was constructed at Etches Park in 1964. Distinct from the carriage depot on the site, the shed was a similar design to those at Burton-on-Trent and Saltley. Etches Park was a 15-minute walk from Derby station and the only time I visited was on the day of the 1978 Derby Works open day, when access was freely granted. The shed was demolished in 2007.

Above: Spotters wander round Etches Park diesel depot on 5 August 1978, having spilled over from the adjacent Locomotive Works' open day. 25300 was the only locomotive on shed that day.

Above: In addition to the refuelling shed, there were several tracks at Etches Park where locomotives could be seen stabled. On 14 May 1984, 20215 was found among three other unidentified Class 20s, with a 31, a 25 and 40015 to their right.

LEICESTER

Above: British Rail's (BR) Leicester depot was on the eastern side of the Midland Main Line; it was visible from the northern end of the station and could be reached by a 15-minute walk. I never formally visited the depot because most locomotives could be seen from passing trains, except of course when a freight train blocked the view, as was the case on 2 June 1980. 45112 arrives with an Up express, whilst 45069 is held on the slow lines. Behind the trains is the depot at Leicester, which was largely made up of unsheltered sidings after the demolition of the steam roundhouse in 1970. When this photograph was taken, the depot only had an allocation of a handful of Class 08 shunters. Two major stabling points linked to the depot were Wellingborough and Coalville, both of which supported the carriage of coal.

Above: The stabling point at Coalville centred on the former goods shed, but with Burton-on-Trent to the west and Leicester to the east, there were no fuelling facilities. Until the collapse of coal mining in the area, the depot often held a dozen locomotives at weekends. By 27 June 1983, when this view was taken, things were very much in decline. 20177 (nearest), 20192, 20084 & 20143 are seen next to the goods shed. The stabling point finally closed in 1990 and very little trace of it exists now. There is currently very little traffic along the Leicester to Burton line, although it now looks likely that passenger services will return on the route.

Below left: The stabling point at Wellingborough was a hangover from the days when it acted as a locomotive changing point for the massive flows of coal traffic from the Midlands to London, where it was consumed by the capital's gasworks and domestic properties. The diesel depot opened in 1965, but by the time of this view, taken on 26 July 1979, it only saw a few locomotives visit each 24 hours. 56059, which was only a few weeks old at the time, was being used for crew training, ahead of the class working the MGR coal trains to Northfleet Cement Works on BR's Southern Region.

BESCOT SHED AND YARD

A three-road diesel depot was built in 1967 on the site of the former steam depot at Bescot. It was an important freight depot throughout the 1970s and 1980s, but with the introduction of the Class 66s in the 1990s and their maintenance being concentrated at Toton, it became less important. The original diesel depot was replaced by a smaller prefabricated structure in 2015. The depot was adjacent to the station and could be reached via a footpath to its north. Most locomotives were visible from the station so it was rarely necessary to walk over to the shed itself. In addition, large numbers of locomotives would be stabled in the former Up Arrival Sidings which had a conveniently located footpath beside them, from which pictures and numbers could be taken. Other places where Bescot's motive power was stabled included Stourbridge Junction and Wolverhampton.

Class	Locos on 7 January 1974	Locos on 6 July 1974
08	3116, 3927 & 3979	08091, 08124, 08294, 08327, 08588, 08590, 08595 & 08812
20	8001 & 20199	20153, 20170 & 20190
24	5085	24038 & 24061
25	5189, 5275, 7562, 7579, 7598, 7606, 7614, 7615, 7630, 7631 & 25208	25117, 25126, 25127, 25188, 25206, 25261, 25263, 25269, 25273 & 25280
45	None	41, 95 & 45002
47	1584, 1676, 1694, 1700, 1868, 1956, 47202 & 47350	47038, 47048, 47105, 47224, 47232, 47306, 47330, 47333, 47335, 47340, 47341, 47450 & 47490

Table 6: Locos present at Bescot on two dates during 1974. It is interesting to note that at the start of 1974 few locos carried TOPS numbers, whereas six months later almost all been renumbered.

Above: Taken from the internal footbridge that linked the Up Yard office with the Down Hump Tower, this image shows the yard stabling point on 23 February 1985, when it contained 20054, 20025, 20005, 20211, 20006, 20073, 20219, 20212, 20001, 20146, 86036, 47328, 47243, 47331, 47307, 58015, 31185 and 25213. The Class 20s were used mainly on local coal traffic from the mines in Staffordshire.

Below: On 30 March 1985 I was allowed an official visit to Bescot, in order to prepare one of my early articles for Rail Enthusiast magazine. The line-up outside the diesel depot was, from left to right, 45029, 47540, 56078, behind which sit 47190 & 25266. In front of the main shed are 08832, 47321, 45020 and 31128.

Above: Several spotters can be seen collecting the numbers in Bescot Yard stabling point on 23 June 1985. From left to right are 20141 (with 20077 coupled to it and 25325 behind the 20s – both out of sight), 45056, 86005, 56063 and 47059.

Above: Looking north with the M6 motorway visible in the background sees 20029, 20228, 20102, 20025, 20035, 20042 & 20072 in the yard stabling point, with 37058 to their right. Taken on 13 February 1991, the Class 20s had been granted a new lease of life, working on departmental trains connected with electrification work in the west midlands.

SALTLEY

The depot was only a 5-minute walk from Duddeston station and although the staff were not necessarily welcoming, it was relatively easy to get round the depot, especially under the cover of darkness! The diesel refuelling shed opened in 1965 and had three covered roads. The depot itself was predominantly a refuelling facility and never had a significant allocation of main line diesels to maintain. Sited at the crossroads of England, it was however very busy with both passenger and freight engines. The loss of locomotive haulage on many of the cross-country services during the late 1980s greatly reduced its work, as did the loss of freight traffic during the late 1980s and early 1990s. The depot eventually closed in 2005 and was demolished in 2008. Table 7 shows a typical weekend line up from the early 1970s.

Class	Locos
08	3020, 3709, 3951 & 3974
25	5167, 5183, 5188, 5190, 5220, 5254, 5261, 7537, 7542, 7601, 7612, 7617, 7640 & 7642
31	5634 & 5690
45–46	68, 99, 114, 117, 128, 129, 142, 159, 162 & 177
47	1544, 1551, 1576, 1625, 1686, 1690, 1825, 47245, 47346, 47348 & 47447

Table 7: Locos present at Saltley on 7 January 1974.

Left, top & above: As mentioned above, most of my visits in the 1970s and '80s to Saltley were during darkness, largely because it was a depot I visited on the way back to Cardiff after a day out further north. On 20 August 1993, I did however manage a daylight visit and took these three images. 47237 & 47223 were found resting near the three-road refuelling shed that had been built to the same design as other Midland Region buildings, such as that at Burton-on-Trent. Four other 47s and a 37 were also visible and by this date the shed was looking a little worse for wear. At the other end of the depot, from left to right are 47971, 47555, 31178, 31102 & 31106 (all in departmental "Dutch" livery), 47286, 37075 and two further 47s on the right – 47476 "Night Mail" and 47707 in Network Southeast livery. The final image shows 58050 and 58028 parked adjacent to the "foreman's chair", a feature I recall from as long ago as 1973 and one of the reasons that it was so difficult to get round the depot during daylight hours!

WORCESTER

The depot at Worcester was a 15 minute walk from Shrub Hill station. I visited it often during 1985 as I found myself working at the nearby Ronkswood Hospital in Worcester for six months. The old three-road steam shed north of the station was modified for diesels in 1966, with the addition of a new roof. The rest of the steam buildings were demolished. The depot gained diesel allocations from Hereford and Bromsgrove in 1964 when those two depots closed, although they both remained active as stabling points. The diesel depot lost its allocation of shunting locomotives in 1978 when it was downgraded to a fuelling point. The roof over the three-road shed was removed, as it became unsafe and the site gradually fell into dereliction. Around 2000 the site was cleared and the area formerly occupied by the diesel depot now has sidings that are used for stabling DMUs.

Above: The semi-derelict former diesel depot at Worcester is well illustrated in this view taken on 25 April 1985. One road has a breeze block wall shutting it off, the next is a dead end siding which had been used for heavier maintenance work and finally a Class 116 DMU headed by vehicle 53888 stands on the only through siding. The roof is long gone and buddleia can be seen sprouting from the supporting walls.

Above: On a dreary 15 July 1985, the six holding sidings alongside the former maintenance shed at Worcester contain 08479, 47152, 47111 and 31164.

Above: Well into the 1980s, Hereford still had a small stabling point to the north of the station. The dual braked Hereford goods pilot 08940 is seen alongside 47187 and 47033. Taken on 5 April 1985, this was a time when some long-distance freight flows along the Marches Line were re-manned at Hereford and there was still local Speedlink traffic from the goods yard and nearby Bulmers Cider factory.

Below: On 19 March 1985, 47223 in engaged in shunting at Bromsgrove's oil terminal. Stabled at the fuelling point are 37221 & 37182, which were the banking locomotives for the nearby steeply-graded Lickey incline.

GLOUCESTER

The depot at Gloucester was a 15-minute walk from Gloucester station, but could also be viewed clearly from the top floor of the Gloucester Royal infirmary where I had a surgical attachment in 1983! The main steam sheds at Gloucester were demolished in the 1960s and a single-track diesel maintenance depot was constructed from the former single-track steam workshop. Most of the tracks to the other sheds were retained and used for stabling locomotives. The depot closed as a maintenance facility in 1991, largely as a result of the withdrawal of Speedlink traffic and the subsequent downgrading of Gloucester New Yard. Locomotives continued to stable at the depot until 1994, after which the site gradually fell into disrepair. The shed still stands in 2023 and there have been suggestions that the depot may be used for a heritage project.

Right: The single road maintenance shed, converted from the former workshop building is seen here on 19 December 1983. 45049 protrudes out of the shed and behind it is an unidentified Class 08 from Gloucester's small allocation.

Below: Four of the stabling sidings, which used to be part of the six-road steam depot, are occupied on 24 November 1983. From left to right are 47239, 31181, 47076 and Class 119 DMU set B581 which consists of vehicles 51059, 59433 & 51102.

Above: One of the busiest scenes I have seen at Gloucester was on 12 August 1984. On the left are 08900, 47559, 31427, with 08781 at the rear of the row. In the distance is 47238, to the right of which is an unidentified 08 and two Class 37s which had been the "Lickey bankers" that week. They had come to Gloucester to stable over the weekend when no freights were scheduled to ascend the incline. To their right 46045 and 47083 can be seen.

LINCOLN

I never made a visit to the site of the depot at Lincoln. This was mainly because it was responsible almost exclusively for DMU maintenance and most of the units could be observed from passing services to Doncaster, Nottingham or March. The three-road maintenance and refuelling shed in Lincoln opened in 1956 and looked after the fleet of Class 114 DMUs that operated the passenger services across most of Lincolnshire.

With the withdrawal of these units, the depot became surplus to requirements and closed in 1987. It then became a maintenance facility for a local bus company, a function that it still fulfils today. There were several stabling points linked to the depot and these included Boston, Grantham and Lincoln East Holmes Yard; these were effectively outposts for shunting locomotives and never held many main line locomotives.

Above: On 12 July 1984 this general view of Lincoln depot was taken from the overbridge at Pelham Crossing. Several two-car Class 114 sets can be seen on shed, as well as the depot pilot 08060.

MARCH WHITEMOOR

The depot at March Whitemoor was perhaps one of the most accessible and friendly depots on the network. Locos stabled at the rear of the depot were easily accessed from the public road and I can't recall ever being thrown out of the shed during the 20 years covered by this book. Just a 20-minute walk from March station, the diesel depot opened in 1963 and serviced predominantly freight locomotives working from the Whitemoor hump yards. After the Down Hump Yard closed, and then the Up Hump in 1980, freight traffic dwindled. The closure of the Speedlink network in 1990/91 led to the loss of what wagonload traffic remained in East Anglia and the depot then became increasingly irrelevant to the modern traffic operations in the area. It closed in 1994 and was demolished in 1996. Some of the land formerly occupied by the depot is now covered by the new Network Rail infrastructure yard that has been built on parts of the old Whitemoor hump yards.

There were two major stabling points for March Whitemoor – Peterborough and Kings Lynn. Both had modern single-track sheds for refuelling and minor repairs. That at Kings Lynn closed in the early 1990s and was demolished in 1994. Peterborough's stabling point survived and continues to be used as a refuelling point.

Class	Locos on 24 Aug 1974	Locos on 10 Jan 1976	Locos on 25 Nov 1978
03	03010	03012	None
08	08026, 08052, 08094, 08096, 08139, 08257, 08438, 08713 & 08827	08026, 08052, 08092, 08096, 08097, 08139, 08257, 08258, 08324, 08427 & 08438	08094, 08096, 08097, 08139, 08209, 08257, 08258 & 08549
20	20032	None	None
25	25125	25169	25271
31	31128, 31174, 31200, 31208, 31210, 31239, 31251 & 31266	31004, 31101, 31154, 31161, 31179, 31204, 31234, 31236, 31240, 31269, 31291, 31315 & 31322	31182, 31206, 31269 & 31405
37	37026, 37028, 37078 & 37109	37014, 37021, 37037, 37043, 37050, 37057, 37059, 37073, 37086, 37101, 37114 & 37120	37025, 37043, 37081, 37097, 37109, 37110, 37114 & 37139
40	40071	None	40067, 40094 & 40164
45–46	46042	None	45056
47	47330	47013 & 47446	

Table 8: Locos present at March Whitemoor on three dates during the 1970s.

Above: On Saturday 4 October 1986 a variety of locomotives and trains are stabled in Lincoln Holmes Yard. On the left 08102 finishes off shunting engineers' wagons for weekend work whilst in the middle is 31107 which had arrived with the 9G09 trip freight from Doncaster Belmont Yard. Stabled on the right are 37202 & 37221 which are on their way from West Burton Power Station to Peterborough with flyash bound for the brick works at Fletton; they will be stabled in the yard until the Monday morning.

These three images were taken at March depot on 1 April 1977 and illustrate classic Eastern Region traction line-ups from the era. The panorama shows from left to right 31322, 31179, 37012, 37036, 37088, 37087 and 40165 which had arrived on a freight from Millerhill. The lower photographs provide us with closeup views of 37051 undergoing minor repairs inside the depot and the same four split headcode 37s that are parked outside. Also present on the depot that day were 08094, 08205, 08324, 08493, 31122, 31262, 37075 and several DMU vehicles.

Above, opposite top & right: Saturday 25 November 1978 was unusual in that three Class 40s were to be found on Whitemoor depot. Three mixed freights from Millerhill, Tyne Yard and Doncaster arrived at Whitemoor Yard between midnight on Friday and lunchtime on Saturday. Often one or two of these would be hauled by a 40, but rarely would all three. 40094 is seen inside the refuelling shed, whilst 40164 has been shunted into the maintenance shed so it can receive minor repairs. Finally 40067, the last to arrive, has been stabled under what remains of the roof of the old steam shed for the weekend, before it returns to Tyne Yard with a mixed freight on the Monday.

Above: This classic view is right next to Hundred Road in March, as seen on 13 June 1991. On the left is withdrawn 45127, with its withdrawn colleagues 45137 and 45132 out of sight behind it. Next to these are 31423, behind which are 31402 and 08518 and 31224 stands on the right. There was no fencing here and often folk wandered into the depot from the road at the weekends.

Above: A few minutes after the shot from Hundred Road, this view was taken as I wandered into the depot. The west end of the main shed is lit up by the evening sun and from left to right are 31239, 08100, 37092 and 08173.

Above: On 9 June 1982 all the doors at the east of the maintenance shed were open revealing this pleasingly symmetrical view of 31207, 08427 and 31246 as they receive attention.

Above: Also during the evening of 9 June 1982, 25080, 25253 and 25139 could be seen stabled at the rear of March depot, with 31313 and 37106 beside them.

Above: On 27 June 1983, from left to right, the west end of the maintenance shed sees 37036, 08493, 37173, 08095 and 08272 lined up.

Above: I'm not sure whether my notes are accurate for my visit to March Whitemoor on 27 June 1986 because they record that depot staff said 20162 was stored at the depot, out of use. However, looking at this image it looks very much as if it is in working order and more likely stabled after having arrived from Toton. Certainly after reviewing the available literature, this suggests it wasn't put into storage until 1987.

Above: On 13 June 1991, the sidings adjacent to Hundred Road are full. From left to right are 31224, 31423, 31402, 45137, 45132 and 45127 which is out of sight behind the 31s (the Peaks were all stored). Two of the Class 45s were eventually cut up in Glasgow while the third (45127) was sold to Pete Waterman for spares.

Above: 08705 is the solitary resident of the maintenance shed at March on 13 March 1991.

TRACTION MAINTENANCE DEPOTS

Above: Also on 13 March 1991, 45013 heads a row of six stored Class 45s in the area that used to be part of March's old steam depot.

Above: On the extreme right is a young Phil Sutton, a former railway magazine editor and now the owner of Sutton's Locomotive Workshop, who is seen readying his camera to capture the scene at Whitemoor on 13 June 1991. From left to right are 31434, 31135, 31186, 31181 and a railfreight-liveried 37/0.

Above: One final shot of the depot at Whitemoor on 13 June 1991. 37029 & 37107, both in Railfreight Distribution livery, sit alongside half a dozen 31s at the west end of the depot area. On the right are some of the stored locomotives stabled on the site of the old steam shed.

Above: As well as the refuelling shed at King's Lynn, locomotives often used the sidings to the east of the main station to stable during weekends. On 3 November 1979, 08324 is joined by 37259 and 37054. The masses of sand between the rails are because locomotives on trains from the nearby sand terminal at Middleton Towers would run round in this area.

Above: In between duties on the King's Lynn Dock branch, 03175 and 03017 are stabled in the refuelling point at King's Lynn on 2 June 1981.

Above: On 6 October 1979, 31218, 31132 and 31224 are stabled just north of Peterborough station. The single-track fuelling shed is just out of shot to the left of this view.

Above: As well as stabling to the north of Peterborough station, locomotives would often also be stabled at the station itself during weekends. Such was the case on 3 February 1990, when 08705, 08713 and 08529 were parked next to Peterborough's Royal Mail sorting office.

Class	Locos
08	08272, 08315, 08324, 08339, 08406, 08412 & 08413
25	25116 & 25130
31	31108, 31159, 31179, 31195, 31207, 31219 & 31226
46	46040

Table 9: Locos that were present at Peterborough on 24 August 1974.

NORWICH

Norwich Thorpe depot consisted of the converted steam sheds and a new DMU servicing building. It opened in 1956 and was just a ten-minute walk from the station. My notes suggest I received a friendly reception on my visits and it seems I was welcomed both into the depot and several of the signal boxes that controlled access to the depot and the adjacent goods yards. The depot had two stabling points which were at Yarmouth and Lowestoft. Visits to these during the 1970s only ever found the Class 03s that worked in the dock areas of these two ports. The "make do and mend" facilities at Norwich were replaced by a

new purpose-built modern servicing depot on the former goods yard at Wensum Junction. This was named Crown Point and opened in 1982 with a total of 26 sidings, seven of which were under cover, making it a sizeable depot. After resignalling and electrification in 1986, the depot serviced the Class 86s and later the Class 90s that worked the express passenger trains to London. After significant recent investment, the depot now services the new Stadler multiple units that have begun working passenger services across much of East Anglia, making the depot the largest in the region.

Below & right: On 20 December 1975, I was on my way from Cardiff to catch the overnight ferry to Hoek van Holland in order to visit my German pen friend near Betzdorf and I took a diversion to visit Norwich, Yarmouth and Lowestoft. I found 31317 at the west end of the old steam sheds at Norwich Thorpe. Also present on shed that day were 03018, 03020, 03029, 03034, 03037, 03045, 03103, 31161, 31216, 31251, 31305, 31318, 37033, 37038, 37043, 47150 and a dozen or so DMU carriages. Interestingly, I also noted 03050 in Crown Point Yard, which at this date was still a general goods marshalling yard. Alongside the yard pilot were three withdrawn Class 17 Claytons. Sadly I did not note their numbers. In order to try and "cop" all the Norwich-based Class 03s in one visit I then travelled from Norwich to Yarmouth and Lowestoft. 03370 was found at the buffer stops at Yarmouth, in a station that looks completely different to how it appears today. 03035 was also stabled at the station, whilst at Lowestoft 03062 was present. The day was then rounded off with a visit to Ipswich which yielded another seven 03s stabled next to the station. Finally three more of the class were found at Colchester, before the trip to Parkeston Quay and the ferry trip to Europe. Whilst the quality of these two images isn't as strong as the rest in this book, they have been included because photos of the old steam shed at Norwich Thorpe and Great Yarmouth station before its roof was removed are uncommon.

Right: On 8 June 1979, 37092 stands at the east end of the four-road steam depot at Norwich Thorpe, which had been converted for use by diesels during the late 1950s.

Above: The two-track carriage shed at Norwich Crown Point was designed to accommodate a locomotive and a full rake of coaches, such as those used on passenger services to London Liverpool Street. On 19 December 1991, in InterCity livery, 86218 stands within the depot with an incomplete set of the Mark 2 coaches used on London trains.

Below: Crown Point only ever had an allocation of shunting locomotives and was mainly a centre for maintaining the DMUs used on the branch lines of East Anglia. On 19 December 1991, 08658, 08868, 08685 and 08936 line up at the rear of the depot.

SOUTHERN ENGLAND

CAMBRIDGE

The diesel depot, which opened in 1958 primarily to service DMUs, is a 25-minute walk from the station. I never undertook this walk as most locomotives were stabled at Cambridge station and by the time I did visit the depot, I was a student in Cambridge and could cycle directly there. I also visited the signal box at Coldhams Lane which controlled access to the depot and provided good overall views of the complex. The small locomotive servicing shed to the east of the site was easy to reach without being noticed by the main office staff and I popped in there a few times when I was a student. The depot closed in 1996, however after a period of inactivity it has been used by several private companies in recent times and is currently used by Govia Thameslink Railway.

Above: On 7 October 1978, two Class 101 DMUs consisting of vehicles 56377, 51225, 51212 & 56373 stand in the main servicing shed at Cambridge. Just visible behind these is 08716.

On 8 May 1979, pilot scheme loco 31004 was found stabled at the north end of Cambridge station.

Left & opposite bottom left: On 9 May 1979, 47184 had just been repainted and the name "County of Cambridgeshire" applied by Stratford depot's fitters. The locomotive is seen at Cambridge depot prior to the official naming ceremony, with the nameplates still covered. Also present were the more mundane residents 08052 and 08207.

Above: By the 1980s, Cambridge only had an allocation of a handful of Class 08s, three of which were allocated to work in the nearby yard and station area. On 18 November 1980, 08052, 08418 and 08863 were all stabled in the yard at Cambridge.

Above: The stabling points for Cambridge depot included Cambridge Station, Chesterton Junction and Bury St Edmunds. On 27 April 1980 the station stabling point is host to three Class 37s, two 31s and a 47, most of which were used on the passenger services from Cambridge to London's Liverpool Street and King's Cross stations.

Above: Taken from Coldhams Lane Signal Box on 6 May 1981, this view shows a Class 101 (vehicles 51444 & 56377) just before it left the depot for the short journey to Cambridge station. Several other DMUs and at least two 08s are also visible.

COLCHESTER

The depot at Colchester was a 5-minute walk from the station, but an attempt to trespass was rarely necessary because the locomotives on shed could usually be seen and photographed from the station's long platform. The facility opened in 1961, but by the 1970s and 1980s it generally didn't contain more than three or four locomotives. It has survived into the 21st century and is now used to service multiple units. According the 1972 Locoshed Directory, the two stabling points linked to Colchester were Harwich Parkeston Quay and Ipswich.

During the 1970s, Harwich was by far the busier stabling point, as the train ferry traffic generated at least half a dozen daily Speedlink workings. After train ferry operations ceased in 1986 the importance of the railway yards at Harwich was greatly reduced, as was that of the stabling point there. In contrast, the rise of container services from Felixstowe led to more and more locomotives using the stabling point adjacent to Ipswich station and this became the busiest stabling point in East Anglia in the 1990s.

Above: 47255 arrives at Colchester with a London Liverpool Street to Norwich express on 10 December 1979. To the right of the train, on shed that day were 31212, 47323 and an unidentified Class 37.

Above: The driver and secondman prepare to start up 31212, which along with 47323 had received minor attention at Colchester depot earlier in the day on 10 December 1979. The funnel of the train ferry is visible above 47323, which later took a Speedlink service to Whitemoor Yard. Also stabled at Parkeston Quay that day were 47016 and 08228.

Above: On 2 June 1984, at a pre-electrification Ipswich station, the stabling point holds 03399 which was one of the Class 03s used to shunt the yard and Docks branch in Ipswich. Also visible are 31420 and 37001; the Class 37 is coupled to a sister locomotive and together they would be used on a Felixstowe to Trafford Park freightliner service later in the day. A two-car Class 105, which consists of vehicles 54422 & 51268, is awaiting departure with one of the hourly Ipswich to Cambridge services.

Above: Ipswich was the site of one of the earliest diesel depots. It was built in 1954, but had been abandoned by this time this view of 86236 was captured, as it passes the semi-derelict buildings with a Norwich to Liverpool Street express on 7 September 1987. This location is to the west of Ipswich station and the buildings remained standing until 1991.

Below: The increasing importance of Ipswich during the 1990s is reflected in this view from 6 June 1996. High horsepower diesel and electric traction dominates as the number of freightliner services from Felixstowe continued to increase. From left to right are 08745, 56081, 56097, an unidentified Class 56 in "Dutch" Civil Engineers livery, an unidentified 86, 90146 and 86635.

HITCHIN

The depot at Hitchin was only a five minute-walk from the station. Opened in 1961, it was designed to look after the small fleet of Class 31s used on suburban services out of King's Cross, as well as a handful of shunting locomotives. With electrification to Hitchin, the depot lost most of its "raison d'etre" and no longer had a locomotive allocation from 1978. It continued as a permanent way depot for a couple of decades and even though the rails to the shed were removed in 2012, the building was still standing in 2022.

Above: On 3 April 1976 (a Saturday), most of Hitchin's engines were to be found on shed. 31171 heads a line of six 31s, with two more on the shed roads. The other seven 31s were 31183, 31186, 31190, 31209, 31218, 31223 & 31227 and 08545, 08549 & 08550 were also present that day.

Above: On 10 March 1978, a solitary 31199 stands outside the two-road shed at Hitchin.

CRICKLEWOOD

The depot was a short walk north of Cricklewood station and was a place I only ever visited once, in February 1975. I suspect this was because there tended to be relatively few locomotives stabled there, but also because many of these could also be seen at locations further north, such as at Toton which was a favourite destination in the 1970s. Whatever the reason, like most of my trainspotting trips to London, the visit took place on a Saturday during the winter months because that was when special day return offers were available, allowing cheaper than normal tickets to the capital. That did mean that my photography was quite restricted though, as the shed visits were often after dark! The new diesel depot at Cricklewood opened in 1960 and was

designed to cater for both locomotives and DMUs. For various reasons, the extensive facilities for locomotives were never fully utilised and when suburban services to Bedford were first operated by electric trains in 1977, less than 50 locomotives were allocated to Cricklewood. The introduction of HSTs on the passenger expresses from St Pancras in 1982 sounded the death knell for the depot's locomotive allocation and by 1987 it had ceased carrying out locomotive maintenance. Cricklewood depot closed in 1988 and was demolished in 1992. The main stabling point for the depot then became Cambridge Street Sidings, just north of St Pancras. Table 10 summarises the locomotives that were present during my 8 February 1975 visit.

Class	Locos
08	08199, 08235, 08236, 08458, 08535 & 08890
25	25081, 25182, 25250 & 25316
31	31418, 31419, 31420, 31421, 31423 & 31424
45–46	64, 68, 45004, 45042, 45062, 45104, 45125, 45130, 45139, 45140, 45141, 45148 & 46052
47	47004, 47156 & 47204

Table 10: Locos present at Cricklewood on 8 February 1975. In addition there were 76 DMU carriages on shed.

Above: 45148 & 45062 stand at the south end of Cricklewood's heavy maintenance shed on 8 February 1975. 45148 has the headcode 1C16 which I recall was for an express to Nottingham, whilst 45062 has the headcode 7O15 which was a loaded MGR working from Toton to Northfleet.

Right: In 1975, prior to electrification of the line through Cricklewood, suburban services from several London termini relied on Class 31s. 31423, 31424 & 31420 are stabled at Cricklewood on Saturday 8 February 1975 ahead of them being assigned to passenger trains that would begin at Bedford the following Monday morning.

FINSBURY PARK

Finsbury Park depot was a ten-minute walk from the passenger station of the same name. Whilst I did manage several visits, I was singularly unsuccessful at getting any decent photographs of the place! This was mainly because it was very strict and I got booted out several times and the only occasions that I managed to collect all the numbers were after dark. There is one very poor blurred image of a Class 40 far from the main shed in my collection, but unfortunately it isn't good enough to reproduce here. The depot opened in 1960 with an impressive six-road maintenance shed. Its demise came in the early 1980s, when the Class 55 "Deltics" were withdrawn from East Coast Main Line passenger services and

replaced by HSTs which were based at the nearby Bounds Green depot. Finsbury Park closed as a maintenance depot in 1981 and as a fuelling point in 1983. The land was eventually given over to housing and somewhat amusingly, my brother's first flat was on the site of the former depot! The main stabling point for Finsbury Park's motive power was York Way, which was located immediately north of the platforms at King's Cross. This had a single-road servicing shed and five further stabling sidings until 1979, when a combination of electrification of the suburban services and the use of HSTs rendered the facility surplus to requirements. Table 11 lists a typical line up at Finsbury Park, as found during a dusk visit in 1974.

Class	Locos
08	3086, 08528, 08550, 08553, 08556, 08558 & 08872
31	5543, 5544, 5606, 5610, 5612, 5614, 5618, 5633, 5641, 5644, 5652, 5657, 5662, 5834, 5859, 31152, 31183, 31199, 31207, 31238, 31249, 31268 & 31401
40	40074 & 40149
46	46044 & 46055
47	47051, 47144, 47303, 47408, 47409, 47410, 47411 & 47479
55	55015 & 55021

Table 11: Locos present at Finsbury Park on 23 February 1974.

Above: This image captures the excitement as one trotted along Platforms 8 & 9 at King's Cross during the 1970s. The stabling point at York Way can be seen in the distance and on 23 February 1974 this contained from left to right Class 31 5605, 47403, 47050, 31178, 55018 and 55012, behind which 46036 is just visible. In the refuelling shed to the right of these is 47412. The crowd of spotters at the end of the platform are a reminder of how popular the hobby was, even though more than five years had passed since steam ended in 1968.

Above: 55016 "GORDON HIGHLANDER" is seen adjacent to the single-track refuelling shed at York Way stabling point on 19 April 1977, while one of the staff enjoys the spring sun between refuelling duties.

Below: On 19 December 1975, 55001 "ST. PADDY" rests at York Way in the last light of the day.

STRATFORD

The traction maintenance depot at Stratford was a favourite spot to visit both because the staff were always friendly (in contrast to Finsbury Park for example) and because out of all the London depots, it held by far the largest number of locomotives, with at least 70 present most weekends. It was easily reached by a ten-minute walk through a lengthy pedestrian tunnel from Stratford station. The view upon exiting the tunnel was one of the most exciting in my shed bashing days and I have therefore included an old black and white picture of it. The depot dates back to 1840 and as early as 1957, alterations were made to accommodate the first diesels as they began to arrive. The main diesel depot opened in 1958, with a purpose built four-track maintenance building and separate facilities for refuelling and the care of DMUs. The area previously used as the locomotive works closed in 1991, which during its lifetime had been used to repair everything from steam locomotives, to Deltics and Class 86 electrics. The main depot then fell victim to privatisation, as it handled mainly freight motive power and so when the majority of this was reallocated to Toton depot, it ceased to have a purpose and closed in 2001.

The whole area, including the former freightliner depot to the north of the depot complex, later became the Olympic Park for the 2012 London Olympic Games. Table 12 gives a sample of the number and variety of locomotives that could be found at Stratford on a typical Saturday during the 1970s, in this case there were 98 engines on shed.

There were two stabling points linked to the depot. The first was at Ripple Lane, where a modern diesel depot opened in 1958. This was part of the new Ripple Lane Hump Yard and serviced the freight locomotives that were used on the petrochemical and automotive related freights which ran along the former London Tilbury & Southend lines. The hump yard at Ripple Lane was one of the earliest casualties of BR's Modernisation Plan and closed in 1970. The diesel servicing depot at Ripple Lane however, survived until 1994 when it closed, to be demolished three years later in 1997. The second stabling point linked to Stratford was Liverpool Steet station, where there was a refuelling facility that prevented passenger locomotives having to travel all the way to Stratford and back in order to refuel.

Class	Locos
03	2164 & 2168
08	3069, 3075, 3112, 3176, 3248, 3301, 3302, 3309, 3311, 3339, 3523, 3524, 3537, 3673, 3681, 3683, 3684, 3705, 3716, 3865, 3917 & 4191
31	5500, 5501, 5502, 5503, 5504, 5505, 5506, 5507, 5508, 5510, 5512, 5513, 5514, 5515, 5516, 5517, 5521, 5547, 5552, 5553, 5568, 5569, 5576, 5598, 5610, 5618, 5631, 5635, 5646, 5653, 5679, 5681, 5697, 5802, 5812, 5825 & 5847
37	6704, 6711, 6728, 6734, 6739, 6744, 6753, 6783, 6811, 6819, 6820, 6830, 6915, 6950, 6959, 6965 & 6966
46	169
47	1110, 1526, 1529, 1572, 1654, 1695, 1715, 1717, 1748, 1749, 1751, 1758, 1765, 1774, 1820, 1947, 1953, 47118 & 47401

Table 12: The locos that were present at Stratford on 17 November 1973, when an impressive selection of 24 diesel shunters, 37 Class 31s, 20 Class 37s and 19 Class 47s were all visible.

Above: On 6 December 1977 the heavy maintenance shed at Stratford is almost full. From left to right are 47543, 31103, 37263, 47155 and 47003.

On 8 February 1975 there were a total of 86 locomotives and 46 DMUs on shed at Stratford. 31012 is seen at the head of a row of fellow pilot scheme Type 2s, which includes 31018, 31009, 31005, 31001, 31004, 31011 & 31015 to the south of the main maintenance shed. The second image, which among other locos shows 31013, 31314 and 37014, is the view that greeted the visitor upon emerging from the pedestrian tunnel at Stratford. These are the tracks that led to the unrefurbished steam shed in the early 1970s. Finally 37012 is seen at the head of another row of stabled locomotives, with a second unidentified Class 37 visible outside the west end of the main shed at Stratford.

Above: On 6 September 1976, there were 79 locos on shed that day including 45007 and 37041 which were visible at the east end of the maintenance building.

Above: The Works at Stratford repaired a wide range of motive power, including Class 86 electrics and Class 55 "Deltics", as this image taken on 4 December 1980 reveals. After having been lifted off its bogies, 55005 "THE PRINCE OF WALES'S OWN REGIMENT OF YORKSHIRE" stands alongside an unidentified Class 31 within the shops.

Right: On Saturday 6 September 1976 Stratford Depot was packed, with 101 locomotives and DMUs on shed. 37041 stands at the eastern end of the refuelling shed; on the depot that day were ten other Class 37s, 25 Class 31s, 24 Class 08s, 15 Class 47s and a visiting Class 45 and Class 40, both of which had arrived from the north via Whitemoor to Temple Mills freight services.

Above: These two views were taken on 6 December 1977 at the former locomotive building works, which were located to the north of Stratford's main diesel depot buildings. Inside the four-track workshop that day were an unidentified Class 47 on the left, 47493 which is being lifted off its bogies by a 50-ton crane, with 31279 behind and 31405 to the right. Outside are 37127 & 37057 (note the collision damage on the latter) and 31012 which had been withdrawn from service the preceding year. 08724 and a variety of other vehicles keep them company at the eastern end of the works building.

‖ **Above:** On 21 July 1991, 86401 is undergoing a general overhaul in "the Works" which closed later that year.

Above: My notes record that this image of Ripple Lane depot was taken on 400 ASA film with an exposure of 1/30 at f4. The lighting was dire on 28 November 1989, when I took what is my only picture of Ripple Lane. From left to right, the locomotives facing the camera are 47283, 47345 and 37890.

Below: Even though the station had been electrified, diesels clearly dominate this scene at London Liverpool Street on 16 February 1981. The fuelling point usually held a couple of passenger or parcel locomotives, as well as providing a siding for the Class 08 station pilot. The stabling point and station are busy with from left to right 31204, behind which is an unidentified Class 47 and some fuel oil tanks. Next is 47581 with its signature Stratford depot silver roof, then another 47 and an 08 in the depths of the station, followed by 47557 on a Norwich-bound express. Finally on the right is 31326 with a Cambridge service, which I was about to catch.

OLD OAK COMMON

The depot at Old Oak Common was a 15-minute walk from Willesden Junction station. It opened in 1965 after the steam depot on the same site closed in 1964. The old steam era workshops were converted into a seven-track building for the heavy maintenance of diesels and a three-track servicing and refuelling building was tacked onto a steam era turntable, which was retained for stabling diesel locomotives. It could be said that in comparison to the purpose-built diesel depots at Cardiff Canton and Plymouth Laira, Old Oak Common was a bit of a "bodged job"! The depot survived into the privatisation era, but eventually closed in 2018 and was then demolished to make way for the massive 42-track Elizabeth Line London Underground depot. Table 13 gives an idea of the variety of Western Region traction that could be found at the depot during the 1970s.

Class	Locos on 23 February 1974	Locos on 10 March 1979
08	08484, 08630, 08785, 08786, 08787, 08795, 08798, 08936, 08947, 08949 & 08950	08480, 08656, 08793 & 08947
31	5535, 5685, 5690, 5809, 31118, 31259 & 31295	31117, 31132, 31135, 31163, 31181, 31209, 31230, 31241 & 31265
35	7000, 7001, 7029, 7031 & 7032	None
47	1599, 1651, 1661, 1901, 1947, 47030, 47056, 47063, 47069, 47070, 47078, 47085, 47089, 47093, 47230, 47240, 47246, 47447, 47470, 47494 & 47506	47024, 47054, 47081, 47128, 47212, 47249, 47295, 47335, 47482, 47509 & 47511
50	402	50045
52	1010, 1011 & 1037	None

Table 13: Locos present at Old Oak Common on two dates during the 1970s.

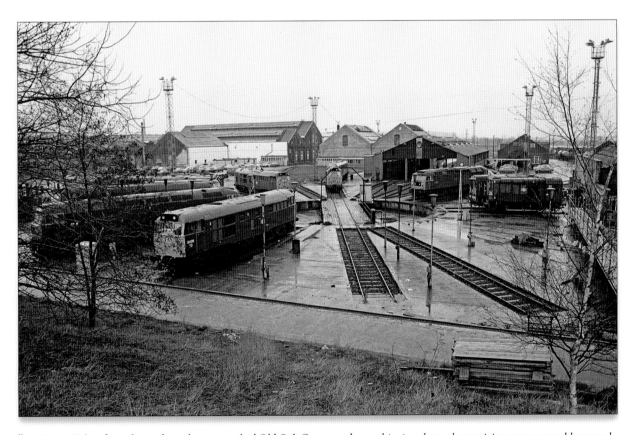

Above: Taken from the roadway that approached Old Oak Common depot, this view shows the surviving steam turntable around which the following locomotives were recorded: 31135, 47111, 31132, 47128, 08483 and 08480. Behind 31135 is the old steam workshop which was known as the factory and to its right is the three-road rapid inspection and refuelling shed. The date was 10 March 1979 and a complete list of locos found at the depot that day is given in Table 13.

ǀǀ **Above:** Inside the cavernous factory on 10 March 1979 were 47509 and 31230.

OXFORD

After demolition of the steam shed in Oxford, a small fuelling facility was built on the site with a two-road refuelling canopy. This was a ten-minute walk from the station and the locomotives stabled there were usually visible from the adjacent public right of way. By the 1980s, Oxford, along with Didcot, was classified as a stabling point for the main depot at Reading. The reduced need for shunting locomotives, the nearby facilities at Reading and the abolition of locomotive-hauled passenger services led to the closure of the stabling point in 2002 and the fuelling "shed" was demolished in 2005.

Above: On 10 March 1979, the former 24142 was found at Oxford. It had been given the departmental number TDB968009 in 1976 when it became a static carriage heating unit and would be moved to Reading later that year. Beyond the refuelling shed, an unidentified Class 08 can be seen in the background.

Above: On 19 October 1984, 58009 was less than a year old. The powerful Type 5 is stabled at Didcot alongside the yard pilot for that week, which was 08816.

Left: On 11 February 1978, whilst on my way to a German A Level course held at Middleton Stoney, I popped into the depot at Oxford to find 47159, 47190, 47078 (with a damaged cab) and 50022 stabled there.

HITHER GREEN AND OTHER SOUTH LONDON STABLING POINTS

BR's Southern Region was mainly served by EMUs and had far fewer locomotives than the other regions and as a result I did not visit many of its depots more than once. One site that I did reach on several occasions was Hither Green. Only a five-minute walk from Hither Green station, it was the main diesel depot for the Eastern Division of the Southern Region. The six-road building, which dates back to steam days, was used for the maintenance of both diesel locomotives and permanent way equipment. A new refuelling shed was built in 1970 and the depot was the primary maintenance and refuelling facility for the south east part of the erstwhile Southern Region into the

21st century. Although it was demoted to a fuelling point under EWS, it remains in use in 2023.

Locomotives also stabled nearer to London at Bricklayers Arms Goods Depot and further from London at Gillingham, Rochester and Hoo Junction. There were of course other large depots on the Southern Region near to London, but these primarily cared for EMUs and were located at Slade Green, Selhurst and Wimbledon. One depot I visited but sadly never photographed was Stewarts Lane, which became the Southern Region's most important depot within the capital. I did however manage to capture a couple of images at some of its stabling points including Waterloo Station and Clapham Junction.

My only pictures taken at Hither Green show some of the many Class 33s that were stabled there on 23 February 1974. 33047, 33051 and 33064 are all illustrated at the south end of the old steam depot and the complete list of locos present that day is given in Table 14.

Class	Locos on 23 February 1974	Locos on 20 November 1976
08–09	08374 & 08653	08374, 08375, 08653 & 09006
33	33033, 33035, 33040, 33041, 33046, 33049, 33054, 33058, 33065, 33203 & 33212	33035, 33038, 33042, 33047, 33048, 33052, 33057, 33058, 33059, 33060, 33063 & 33203
71	None	71004, 71009, 71013 & 71014
73	73108	73004, 73005, 73101 & 73132

Table 14: Locos present at Hither Green on two dates during the mid-1970s.

Above: Also on 23 February 1974, I visited the stabling point at Waterloo station and photographed 74005 and 74002 there. 08152, 33026, 33107 and 33118 were also at rest nearby, at the western edge of the station.

Above: Selhurst-allocated 09012 is seen on duty at Clapham Junction on 15 April 1977. As well as the resident shunting pilot for the carriage sidings, Clapham Junction often saw Class 33s and Class 73s stabled in the yard between the two halves of the station.

MARYLEBONE

The depot was adjacent to the terminus and was effectively two old three-track carriage sheds that had been refurbished and equipped to look after the DMU fleet that operated passenger trains to Aylesbury and Banbury. The depot closed in 1992 and was then demolished, with all its work transferred to Neasden.

Above: On the left, an Aylesbury-bound service accelerates away from London Marylebone and passes the refuelling point on 20 October 1984. The construction of two refuelling roads and a canopy to shelter staff was the only major addition to the former carriage sheds, which are situated behind the photographer.

Below: Class 115 vehicles 51870, 51885 & 51867 all stand at the buffers within Shed 2 at Marylebone on 20 October 1984.

Above: Also on 20 October 1984, inside Shed 1 at Marylebone, 31168 is stabled awaiting its evening departure after having arrived that morning with 6B04, the Northampton to Aylesbury and Marylebone parcels train.

ASHFORD

Ashford Chart Leacon was a depot that I never visited although it was visible from the main line between Ashford and Tonbridge. I suspect this omission was due to it being a 30-minute walk from the station and only a relatively small locomotive fleet being based there. The depot stabled locomotives at several locations, including adjacent to Ashford station, at Dover Harbour, and at Tonbridge, Faversham and Gillingham.

Above & below: On 9 April 1976, I accompanied my father to a medical meeting in Canterbury and borrowed his Olympus Trip camera to take these two pictures of the stabling points at Ashford station and Dover Marine. At Ashford, 71013 and 71008 are alongside 73103; 33053, 33054 and 33210 were also present. Earlier that day the sun was out at Dover Marine stabling point where there was a solitary 33206.

Left: Remarkably, it was not until 19 March 1997 that I took my first pictures of the stabling point at Tonbridge, in spite of several previous visits. Coincidentally, 73103 was stabled there that day, the same locomotive that I had photographed at Ashford station 21 years earlier.

EASTLEIGH

The depot was a 15-minute walk from Eastleigh station and the route to it passed over a bridge that provided views of the locomotive works and continued along the side of the depot, making access fairly easy in the pre-palisade fencing days. Steam finished at Eastleigh depot in 1967 and the diesel depot was gradually built on the site of the former steam shed. It had an eight-road building, four through roads and four dead end sidings which were accessed from the south side of the complex. Its life as a diesel depot came to an end in 1998, but the buildings and the adjacent stabling sidings are still in use today. Locomotives allocated to the depot were stabled as far afield as Salisbury and Basingstoke as well as closer to Eastleigh at Fratton, Southampton Docks and Redbridge Freightliner Terminal.

Above: On 5 April 1975 33026 stands at the south end of Eastleigh depot in what I understood to be a locomotive testing area after engines had undergone major repairs. The other locomotives that were present on that day are summarised in Table 15.

Class	Locos on 31 July 1973	Locos on 5 April 1975
07	2986, 2987, 2988 & 2993	07001, 07002, 07010, 07011 & 07013
08	3043 & 3472	08200, 08202, 08387, 08831, 08845, 08854, 08929 & 08933
33	6504, 6511, 6514, 6524, 6528, 6542 & 6544	33001, 33009, 33013, 33015, 33017, 33025, 33026, 33029, 33030, 33031, 33056, 33103, 33109, 33110 & 33114
47	1101, 1566, 1610, 1634, 1678, 1731, 1774, 1817, 1919 & 1943	47182 & 47243
73	6007, 6028, 6040 & 6041	73001, 73128 & 73131
74	6101, 6107 & 6108	74001, 74002, 74004, 74008 & 74010

Table 15: Locos present at Eastleigh on two dates during the mid-1970s.

Above: 33020 is seen in the stabling sidings to the west of the main depot buildings at Eastleigh on 27 May 1975. To its left is an unidentified Class 74 and 73115, whilst to its right is 47321. Also present that day were 07001, 07003, 07005, 07006, 07010, 33001, 33007, 33021, 33022, 33101, 33106, 33109, 47475, 73134, 73142, 74003, 74005, 74006 and 74008.

Above: As the depot became less important, the number of locomotives that were stabled and re-manned in the sidings adjacent to Eastleigh station increased. On 26 September 1990 the sidings are busy with from left to right, 08760, 47830, 47258 , 47277, then 47099 standing alone and 47006 & 47094 on the right.

Below: On 27 September 1990, a couple of hours were spent bunking off from the British Society of Gastroeneterology, which was held in Southampton, allowing this image of 47532, 47457 and 47145 "MERDDYN EMRYS" on Eastleigh stabling point to be captured.

BRISTOL BATH ROAD

Rebuilt on the site of the former steam depot and opened in 1962, Bath Road was accessed by a walkway from the end of the platform at Bristol Temple Meads or by making a 10-minute walk from the station entrance. There was also an unmanned path into the back of the depot a couple of minutes further along the Bath Road, a fact that I learned too late to avoid my one and only arrest in an engine shed! In 1973, three of us had gone to Bristol to see the summer Saturday traffic and during a quiet moment had run across the walkway and into Bath Road depot. Little did we know that there was a British Transport policeman watching our every move. He caught us in the maintenance shed and my two friends disappeared behind

me and evidently ran out of the depot via the path at the back of the complex, near the old turntable. I didn't know this route existed so surrendered to the long arm of the law. A few days later the police visited me at home and administered a severe warning. Much to my relief my parents were not unduly angry. It transpired that my father had often wandered round engine sheds in the 1940s with his pals in Lancashire and couldn't see what all the fuss was about! Bath Road depot eventually closed in 1995 and has since been demolished. It had stabling points at Westbury and Taunton and during its heyday, as the images below illustrate, 30 to 40 locomotives could often be found within its shed and the outside stabling sidings.

Class	Locos on 10 April 1974	Locos on 1 July 1978
03	2382 & 03121	03121 & 03382
08	3208, 3517, 3526, 3743, 3811, 3816, 3992, 08089, 08584 & 08888	08185, 08218, 08238, 08358 & 08756
25	5202, 7508, 25059 & 25063	25048 & 25134
31	5530, 5617, 31279 & 31309	31106, 31145, 31323 & 31422
35 & 37	7028 & 6939	None
45–46	101, 124, 147, 152, 45108, 46006, 46007 & 46031	45001, 45022, 45070, 45073 & 46022
47	1603, 47174, 47469, 47486, 47494, 47496 & 47509	47048, 47060, 47074, 47089, 47450, 47452 & 47505
50	405, 50001 & 50011	50012, 50018, 50022, 50039 & 50041
52	1061	None

Table 16: Locos present at Bristol Bath Road on two dates during the 1970s.

Below: This general view taken on 1 July 1978 shows the sidings to the east of the depot's three main sheds. These sheds contained six, three and three sidings respectively, after which were these eight sidings which were used to stable fuel oil tankers, vans containing spare parts and motive power not needing maintenance or refuelling.

Above & Below: Two images of the refuelling or "daily shed" where both DMUs and locomotives were refuelled and examined. On 1 July 1978 four different Class 50s, 50012, 50018, 50021 & 50039, are being refuelled alongside a Class 46 and a Class 47, all of which were utilised on summer Saturday workings to Devon and Cornwall. Nealy six years later, on 4 May 1984, the evening shift sees Class 101 set C811 (vehicles 51801, 59548 & 51519), Class 117 set B433 (vehicles 51371, 59509 & 51413) and Class 119 set B577 (vehicles 51063, 59422 & 51091) being refuelled after working trains from Cardiff, Severn Beach and Weston-super-Mare.

Above & below: The three tracks numbered 10–12 served what we used to call "The Works" which was a high roofed shed, where the maintenance roads were just long enough to accommodate a locomotive or DMU carriage. On 1 July 1978, 50041 is undergoing major repairs, as is a DMU carriage to its left. In the second photograph, which looks from the outside, 45073 & 31422 are seen awaiting repairs on the same date.

Below & right: These two views of the main maintenance shed show Bath Road in 1975 and 1992. In 1975, 31110, 50024, 47125 and 47106 await space in the six-road shed for repairs. My notebook records that on this Saturday evening there were just over 50 locomotives within the depot as well as half a dozen DMU carriages. Fast forward to 19 March 1992 and the depot is already looking a bit run down. The motive power outside the shed reflects the workload it undertook at the time for BR's Railfreight and InterCity sectors. 47317 and 47476 are joined by another InterCity branded Class 47 and at least one HST power car. The loss of Speedlink traffic and the general decline in freight led to freight repair work being transferred to Cardiff Canton and the InterCity work being transferred to the nearby Bristol St Phillips Marsh depot.

LAIRA

Laira has been the most important diesel depot in the South West of England during the era covered by this book and indeed since 1962 when it was opened by BR's Western Region to service its diesel hydraulic fleet. It remains an important depot today, having maintained the HSTs that have operated in the region since they first replaced many of its locomotive hauled trains in 1979. It was a long walk from Plymouth station and I only ever managed one visit in 1976, when I was chasing the last of the Class 52 "Westerns". The depot had two major stabling points at Newton Abbot and Exeter. Newton Abbot had been an important depot and workshop on the Western Region but traffic patterns and centralisation led to its closure in 1982. In contrast, Exeter was left without any covered accommodation at the end of steam, yet the roofless former steam depot was a busy stabling point into the 1980s and received a new covered refuelling point in 1987. It has recently been redeveloped and is now a thriving depot with four sidings and covered accommodation.

Below, right & below right: On On 23 July 1976 Laira depot contained an impressive collection of 40 locomotives – 08140, 08238, 08394, 08488, 08489, 08895, 08937, 08945, 25170, 45053, 46005, 46017, 47012, 47030, 47054, 47081, 47107, 47112, 47123, 47128, 50003, 50004, 50010, 50013, 50023, 50027, 50034, 50045 and Class 52s 1005, 1010, 1015, 1022, 1023, 1034, 1037, 1041, 1043, 1049,1063 & 1065. Pictured outside the maintenance shed (right) are D1022 "WESTERN SENTINEL" and 47123. D1005 "WESTERN VENTURER" stands outside Laira's refuelling shed on 23 July 1976. Finally a general view from the road bridge over the West of England main line gives a good impression of the scale of the site, even with a standard lens, which is all I had in those days! On the left is the three-track refuelling building, very similar in design to that at Bristol Bath Road. Next comes the two-track heavy maintenance building, not dissimilar to the four-track shed at Cardiff Canton. Then comes a three-track maintenance building, with the main line in the bottom right hand corner.

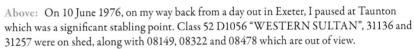

Above: On 10 June 1976, on my way back from a day out in Exeter, I paused at Taunton which was a significant stabling point. Class 52 D1056 "WESTERN SULTAN", 31136 and 31257 were on shed, along with 08149, 08322 and 08478 which are out of view.

Above left: On 23 July 1976 the stabling point at Newton Abbot contained 08091, 08410, 08646, 08955, 31209, 47264, 50018, 50047 and D1051. Sadly my interior shots from that day were blurred and this is my only record of the depot at Newton Abbot, showing D1051 inside the modern diesel servicing shed, alongside 31209.

Left: On 25 September 1984, the servicing point (which was still called a stabling point) at Exeter is busy. From left to right are an unidentified Class 50 and 31309, behind which are a Class 47, a Class 31 and a Class 50, then 31412, 47245 and 50022. By 1984 only a single-track refuelling and servicing shed had been erected, whereas the buildings that have recently been added now provide cover for four roads.

ST BLAZEY

The small depot, dedicated largely to Cornwall's china clay workings, was a ten-minute walk from Par station. Because of a period when our church adventure camps were held in Truro School, this was a depot I visited annually for a few years and always found the welcome friendly. The depot closed to steam in 1962, after which the facilities were largely unchanged as they were used by diesels. The turntable and small semi-roundhouse remained in use until the late 1980s, but the reduced need for locomotive stabling and a drop in freight traffic led to the construction of a small "lean to" servicing shed which replaced these in 1990. That lasted just over a decade, but it too closed as the china clay traffic in Cornwall dwindled such that it only requires a single Class 66 in 2022.

Left: On 17 July 1980, St Blazey's former steam roundhouse contains from left to right, 25057, 37299, 25045 and 46013.

Below: Just over a year later, on 29 July 1981, the depot is housing 47200 against the buffer stops and 37203 & 37142 on one of the turntable approach roads. The trio of 37s visible inside the shed are 37206, 37207 and 37299.

Above: This alternative view of St Blazey depot on 29 July 1983 shows 37270 alongside 46028 and 45038. The Class 46 will later leave with the afternoon Speedlink service to Severn Tunnel Junction which predominantly consisted of china clay that was destined for the north of England and mainland Europe.

Above: On 17 July 1980, 46020 heads away from St Blazey depot with a speedlink service for Acton. The first two vehicles are VIX ferry vans which are conveying china clay from Goonbarrow to Zeebrugge via the Harwich train ferry. Behind these are three further VIX vans from Par Harbour which are destined for Mannheim, Gluckstadt and Basle. The rear of the consist comprises a string of ventilated vans carrying bagged china clay to the B Shed at Swansea Kings Dock which are presumably bound for Ireland..